NOI...

THEN and NOW

A THIRD SELECTION

Philip Standley and Sarah Storey

Photography by Terry Burchell

Foreword by Maggie Secker

John Nickalls Publications

DEDICATION
Dedicated with love and affection to Brian Seager (1934–2003).
A wonderful man who will always be remembered by those who knew him.

PREVIOUS TITLES BY THE AUTHOR
Norwich in Old Picture Postcards Volumes 1, 2, 3 and 4
Norwich – Then and Now
In and Around Norwich – Then and Now

First published in 2003
© 2003 Philip Standley/Sarah Storey
The moral right of the author has been asserted

ISBN 1 904136 11 7

Published by John Nickalls Publications
Oak Farm Bungalow, Sawyers Lane, Suton,
Wymondham, Norfolk, NR18 9SH
Telephone/Fax: 01953 601893

Designed by Ashley Gray and Printed by Geo. R. Reeve Ltd,
9-11 Town Green, Wymondham, Norfolk NR18 0BD
Telephone: 01953 602297

INTRODUCTION

FOLLOWING ON from the success of our two previous volumes, here we are with a third – and who knows, possibly not the last! Each time we publish a book, our friends find yet more early photographs of Norwich, which we feel just have to be published and compared with the modern-day view.

This book begins its journey at Earlham Bridge and visits a few of the surrounding villages before entering the city centre. We take a look at many familiar, and not so familiar, views in the city and finish with a look at each of the grounds of Norwich City Football Club, during its 100-year history.

Within these pages are scenes of the devastating floods of August 1912; in the early hours of Monday 26 August 1912 an incessant torrent of rain began, which continued for the next thirty hours. Across the county the deluge of rain and accompanying gales tore Norfolk apart. Norwich was cut off for the next two days as trams and trains ceased to run, telephone and telegraph lines stopped working, subsidence occurred, bridges collapsed and buildings fell into rivers. Three lives were taken, the most tragic of which was five-month-old Edward Poll who fell from his mother's arms and was swept away. George Brodie of Oak Street died after wading through four-foot-deep water for almost five hours, rescuing several women and children, until he lost his foothold in the strong current. Mrs Kemp of Goat Yard, Oak Street, was the third person to die, with it being reported that she died from 'fright and shock on removal'.

In this book we also see some impressive buildings, which arguably should never have been torn down, but also demolished were run-down dwellings that were little more than slums. Whilst looking at what has been 'lost' we should also note some of the stunning buildings, which replaced these old dwellings, and have survived. Whilst many of these vast alterations took place for the introduction of the tram system of 1900, the trams would only run for 35 years, and the roads that were cut through all those years ago still exist today. Whilst some of the post-war development leaves a lot to be desired, at least with the foresight of photographers like George Swain and George Plunkett, we have been able to record the inevitable changes the city has seen. Isn't it also interesting to look at these old places and try to imagine standing in the same spot a hundred years ago?

An interesting comparison worth noting is the naming of Millennium Plain, by The Forum and Fellowes Plain on the former Norfolk & Norwich Hospital site, which has reintroduced the old tradition of naming open spaces where the streets of Norwich meet as 'Plains'. As time moves on, we still give street names their own local identity acknowledged by most, for example 'Buntings Corner' and 'Jarrolds Corner', whilst the John Lewis store on All Saints' Green is still called 'Bonds' by many folk.

With development continuing across the city, since this book has been written changes to the city are continually being announced, for example Bertram Books of Rosary Road – shown on page 109 – in October 2003 stated they will be moving to the Broadland Business Park and the recent refurbishment and reopening of the Floating Restaurant – shown on page 71 – as a Chinese Floating Restaurant.

This book does not intend to be a definitive history of Norwich but we hope we have highlighted some interesting facts and leave it to you with your own memories to compare the Norwich of yesteryear with that of today. Finally please remember whilst the views of today may not always be considered to be as interesting, perhaps even in as little as twenty years time, you may look at this book again and say; " Do you remember in 2003 when Norwich looked like that?" Today is tomorrow's history and the photographs of our ancestors, present and future generations, all have their place in the history books.

Philip Standley and Sarah Storey
Wymondham 2003

FRONT COVER: Spelmans Horse Sales taken from The Bell Hotel, and the Castle Mall development opened in 1993.
TITLE PAGE: Prince of Wales Road.
BACK COVER: Caleys Advertisement.

ABBREVIATIONS: *c.* (circa) – approximately; *p.u.* – postally used; p.h. – public house.

FOREWORD

So, HERE WE ARE again. Another superb volume of *Norwich – Then and Now; A Third Selection*. Aren't you grateful that there are people who hang on to mementoes from the past – and are prepared to share them with us!

Over the years that I've worked at *BBC Radio Norfolk* I've become increasingly aware of the beauty of the county we live in through the people I've been privileged to meet and chat with. Our City is one of the finest in the country. Parts have changed – no-one could argue with that – and some have miraculously survived for centuries untouched.

The photographs in this volume not only depict changes in certain areas, but also show a very different lifestyle – the age of the horse as opposed to the endless queues of cars!

We are taken through the disaster of the floods, the devastation of war to demolition for the modern age. Still Norwich survives as a 'fine' city.

And how interesting to move to villages on the outskirts. We can see a photograph of what was arguably once one of our grandest halls – Costessey Hall – sadly demolished with very little remaining to remind us of our historic past.

I'm sure you'll never tire of meandering through the pages of this book, comparing 'then and now' and recreating your own visions of the past.

Congratulations to Philip, Sarah and Terry. Hopefully this volume won't be the last.

Maggie Secker
Presenter of 'Maggie's Brew'
BBC Radio Norfolk
(95.1fm 855kHz and 104.4fm 873kHz in the west of the county)

EARLHAM BRIDGE NR NORWICH

THEN – EARLHAM BRIDGE, *p.u.* **1912:** An idyllic scene taken looking away from the city, with youngsters passing their time by the River Yare. This bridge was built in 1774 replacing earlier structures and was constructed of stone with a single arch. Elizabeth Fry (1780–1845), who became a prominent supporter of prison reforms, spent part of her life at the nearby Earlham Hall with her parents John and Catherine Gurney and eleven siblings. Her father John was one of the founders of Gurney's Bank.

NOW: This new Earlham Bridge was constructed in 1963, to the left of the old view. The old bridge became dangerous and was demolished in 1971. Today like all the main approach roads into the city centre, this is very busy with traffic, not only for commuters using the Watton Road but also with the University of East Anglia, and Earlham Park, popular with walkers, close by. This has been exacerbated with the opening in 2001 of the Norfolk and Norwich University Hospital, bringing even more traffic.

THEN – COSTESSEY HALL, *c.* 1910: After the death of Henry VIII, the Jerningham family fought for Mary's right to the throne and in gratitude Mary gave Sir Henry Jerningham the old Tudor Manor House in Costessey. After Mary's death in 1558, Sir Henry decided to have a 'New Hall' built, which was completed in 1564 and extended in about 1800. In 1827, Sir George Jerningham began work on the ornate extension to the New Hall, with his descendants and their tenants continuing to reside here until the early 1900s.

NOW: After the death of The Right Hon. FitzOsbert Jerningham, the Hall closed and the contents were sold in December 1913. The War Office took over the estate during the First World War and after the War, the empty hall was beyond repair and it was sold to a demolition company for £5,000. The Hall was demolished around 1920 and the grounds became a farm and pig-rearing unit until 1984 when it became the home of Costessey Park Golf Club. All that now remains of Costessey Hall is the belfry tower by the 18th fairway.

The Maids Head Inn, Catton, Norwich, Scene of the Inquest Nov. 2nd 1908.

THEN – THE MAID'S HEAD INN, SPIXWORTH ROAD, OLD CATTON: The inquest into the murder of nineteen-year-old Eleanor (Nellie) Howard of Hainford, by her sweetheart Horace Larter of Ber Street, was held here at the Maid's Head Inn on 2 November 1908. The murder had taken place on Spixworth Road with a 1/- clasp knife bought a few days before at Pearson's the cutlers and the body was discovered on the evening of 12 October 1908. Following a verdict of wilful murder, Larter was later sent to Broadmoor.

NOW: Over the last hundred years Old Catton has grown from a village to become a suburb of Norwich, but locals still regard it as a village and it has retained its community spirit. In 1911, the population was 634, whilst in 1999 it was 5,640! Old Catton can proudly boast that it was while Anna Sewell was living at The White House, that she wrote *Black Beauty*. Born in Great Yarmouth in 1820, Anna was crippled when she was a teenager. She died in 1878 unaware of the worldwide success her one and only novel would receive.

SPROWSTON J 9095 (V. J. Buckingham's Series)

THEN – BLUE BOAR PUBLIC HOUSE, WROXHAM ROAD, SPROWSTON, *c.* **1934:** Pictured looking towards the city centre when John Blyth was the landlord, the Blue Boar dates as far back as the late 18th century, when it was owned by St Martin's Brewery. In the 19th century it became a freehouse supplied by Steward & Patteson, before Youngs, Crawshay & Youngs took over. This scene is rather unusual as the Blue Boar sign is on the left-hand side of the road, opposite the pub.   *BASIL GOWEN COLLECTION*

NOW: Where the old pub sign stood is now the junction with Blue Boar Lane, one of the many busy roads on the outskirts of Norwich, and which provides a link to Salhouse Road. Shortly after the earlier photograph was taken, in about 1936, Youngs, Crawshay & Youngs demolished the original Blue Boar public house and new larger premises were built further back from the road out of view of our modern-day photograph. It is still popular, offering hotel accommodation and is renowned for the good food served.

THEN – LAZAR HOUSE, SPROWSTON ROAD, *p.u.* **1907:** The Lazar Hospital, was founded by Bishop Herbert De Losinga early in the 12th century as a hospital for lepers and was known as St Mary Magdalene by Norwich. In 1547, the Hospital closed and by the 18th century it had become virtually a ruined barn, still surrounded by open land. It was saved from further decline in 1902 by Walter Rye and bought in 1906 by Sir Eustace Gurney JP, who restored the building and presented it to the city in May 1921.

NOW: Swallowed up into the suburb of Sprowston, the Lazar House was opened on 6 November 1923 as the first branch library in the city. It housed 5,000 volumes and loaned an average of 164 books each day. In 1989, plans to close the library were dropped when a 2,138 named petition was given to the council. Following a further announcement in 2002 to axe the library, and despite vigorous campaigning, it closed its doors in May 2003, but it is hoped the building will still serve the local community in the future.

THEN – TROWSE, *p.u.* **1923:** Soldiers on horseback are seen passing along The Street. In the background is St Andrew's Church, whose parish registers date back to 1569. Russell James Colman Esq, of Crown Point House, was the lord of the manor and the main landowner. Trowse had its own school, built in 1879, and three public houses – the Crown Point Tavern, the Royal Oak and the White Horse. Numerous shops and trades were in place in the parish, including farmers, a boot repairer, a miller, a blacksmith and a baker.

NOW: Trowse has in recent years been able to regain its village charm thanks to the construction of the bypass in the early 1990s, which has taken away much of the heavy traffic, although the peace is again under threat with a proposed Park & Ride scheme. A poignant reminder of our rural past is still in evidence with the survival of the horse trough by The Common. The view today is very much the same with the only exceptions being the loss of the house on the left and the indications of modern-day living.

THEN – EATON STREET, EATON: A quiet view of this parish taken looking towards Cringleford. On the left-hand corner at the junction with Church Lane stands Eaton Bakery, with its display of pastries and confectionery. Further down the hill the Dutch gables of the Red Lion p.h., built in the late 17th century, can be seen. On the right is Eaton Post Office run in 1912 by Mrs Ann Reeve, who was also advertising and selling Norwich's very own 'Caleys' chocolate. Next-door is the Eaton Working Men's Club.

NOW: The old bakery shop is currently occupied by Elliots of Eaton, a chain of estate agents, whilst the row of cottages on the left are now providing a variety of local services. The old buildings on the right have been demolished, widening the junction with Bluebell Lane, although a Post Office is in existence close by. The Red Lion remains a popular pub with locals and visitors. It is now hard to imagine that until 1975 this formed part of the main Norwich to London A11 road.

THEN – ST STEPHEN'S ROAD, *p.u.* 1905: Looking towards St Stephen's Street, on the left is W Read, cab proprietor, next to a furniture dealer. No. 15 was a chemist's shop, with a general store at No. 13 and a confectioner's next to The Coachmakers Arms p.h., owned by Morgans Brewery, dating back to the 15th century. Next-door is Norman Beard Ltd, organ builders. The Castle is visible in the distance, whilst on the corner of St Stephen's Street and Queen's Road stands the Great Eastern p.h. *COLIN PROCTOR COLLECTION*

NOW: 'Megazone', a laser adventure games complex, once the Gala Ballroom, occupies the site on the left, and the chemist's is an Indian takeaway; a hearing centre and a health and beauty clinic occupy the adjacent premises. In 1937, Moray Smith, an Italian PoW, who had married a Costessey girl and taken her surname, stood on scaffolding and created a new sign here for the Coachmakers' Arms, depicting the old St Stephen's Gate. The view towards St Stephen's Street has vastly altered with the redevelopment of the 1960s.

THEN – SURREY STREET, *c.* **1905:** On the left is the Norwich Union Fire Office and in the distance is the ancient Boar's Head tavern. In 1797, Thomas Bignold, a banker and wine merchant, formed Norwich Union after his experiences of trying to obtain insurance against highwaymen when he had moved to Norwich. Surrey House, designed by George Skipper, with its unique marble hall was opened on 17 December 1904 as the head office of Norwich Union Life Society. *CLIVE MANSON COLLECTION*

NOW: On the left is the entrance to the Bus Station opened in 1936. The old Boar's Head was destroyed in the Blitz of April 1942. The right-hand side is now dominated by the development of Norwich Union offices constructed in the 1950/60s, giving employment to thousands of local people. In 2000 Norwich Union merged with CGU to become CGNU plc and in 2002 was renamed Aviva plc. The name Norwich Union is still retained with an image of the cathedral as its logo, first used in 1877, for its life products and services.

THEN – ALL SAINTS' GREEN, *c.* 1885: An early photograph of the blacksmith's and chimney sweep's premises on the corner of All Saints' Street and All Saints' Green, which apart from the street signs gives no clues to its present-day location. A larger building would be erected here and occupied by a pawnbroker until the devastating air raids of 1942. On Ber Street, Robert H Bond had opened his first drapery shop in 1879 and adjoining properties were soon purchased as his business flourished. *CLIVE MANSON COLLECTION*

NOW: In 1914, Bonds opened the Arcade on All Saints' Green and in 1930 expanded into the Thatched Cinema. By 1939 Bonds employed 200 people and were serving 13,000 customers a day. On 27 June 1942, Hitler's bombs devastated Bonds' stores, but trading soon recommenced in makeshift stores and buses! A new department store was built in the early 1950s, creating the curve from All Saints' Street to All Saints' Green. In the 1980s, the John Lewis Partnership purchased Bonds, and Bonds name was retained until 2001.

WESTLEGATE ST NORWICH. 128. J.H.

THEN – WESTLEGATE, *p.u.* 1909: Once known as Wastel Way, it is hard to imagine that a hundred years ago, Westlegate was little more than this narrow lane with quaint old cottages and houses, running from All Saints' Green to St Stephen's Plain. All Saints' church towered over the former thatched Light Dragoon, 'Barking Dickey', public house. The nickname was gained due to the poorly-drawn pub sign, which resembled a braying donkey rather than the intended Lighthorseman's steed. No. 14, where the horse is preparing for a delivery, was occupied by John De Caux Forwarding Agents and Parcel Express Offices for Fosters, Globe, Carter Paterson & Co Ltd. Charles F Watling, general carriers, removal and haulage contractors would, by the 1920s together with Carter Paterson & Co Ltd, dominate these former stables together with the adjacent properties as far as the 'Barking Dickey' and remained in business until just after World War Two. Further down on the left-hand side, the building with the gas lamp was the home of the Canterbury Tavern, a Morgans public house.

NOW: In March 1965 Williams Deacon's, one of the banks, which later became Williams & Glyn's Bank, opened in the former 'Barking Dickey'. In more recent times the thatched building has become a coffee shop. Westlegate House, known as the 'glass tower', with its distinctive glass shields, was built in the early 1960s on the former Watlings site. This has housed many occupants over the years and in the early 1980s McDonalds opened their first burger bar in the city in the ground floor accommodation. Westlegate was widened in 1925 and it was at this time, after the Canterbury Tavern's closure in 1924, that Deacon's new fish restaurant was built on the corner with Red Lion Street, with the edge of the building just visible here. For the past few years, a sports shop has occupied the premises of Deacon's restaurant. Due to the increasing flow of traffic Westlegate is these days a busy one way, three-lane carriageway.

THEN – RAMPANT HORSE STREET, *c. 1905:* Formerly called the Horse Market the street was renamed after the Rampant Horse Inn, which once stood there. Here on the corner of St Stephen's Street, is Arthur Bunting & Co Ltd, drapery store, which opened in 1866. Bunting's prided themselves on providing quality products at fair prices and their slogan was 'Latest, Cheapest and Best'. Trading next door were Snelling & Sons, confectioners and H Cockerill, hats and fancy goods dealers. *CLIVE MANSON COLLECTION*

NOW: Buntings' store was rebuilt in 1912 to the elegant designs of Augustus Scott, a pioneer in the use of reinforced concrete. In the 'Blitz' of April '42, Buntings was damaged, and they relocated to London Street. However the main façade of the building was saved and it was converted into a luxury NAAFI for the armed forces. After the war, Marks and Spencer took over the site and opened here on 31 March 1950. They have since extended along St Stephen's Street and into the former Woolworths' store on Rampant Horse Street.

THEN – ST PETER MANCROFT FROM THE ASSEMBLY HOUSE, THEATRE STREET, *c.* **1860:** A very early image from the pioneering days of photography looking across Theatre Street and the rooftops of St Peter's Street and Bethel Street. In the foreground the yard of the White Swan, also known as the Swan Inn, located on St Peter's Street is clearly visible. With its White Swan Playhouse the inn was the home of the Norwich Company of Comedians between 1730 until 1758 when Thomas Ivory opened the New Theatre – the first Theatre Royal – close by. The White Swan continued to attract passing shows and later became a centre for cock-fighting and prize-fighting and closed by the end of the 19th century. For many years afterwards wholesale grocers occupied the building.

CLIVE MANSON COLLECTION

NOW: The old houses on St Peter's Street, including the site of the former White Swan, were demolished in the early 1960s for the Bethel Street public car park, which stood in front of the Norwich Central Library. On 1 August 1994, a disastrous fire destroyed the Library. The Forum, which is now the main focus of this view, has arisen from the ashes and was officially opened by Queen Elizabeth II in 2002. The Forum, on Millennium Plain is home to a vast array of facilities, together with being the new home for *BBC Local Radio and Television*. The parish church of St Peter Mancroft still dominates this part of the city centre. This magnificent church was built between 1430 and 1455 in the perpendicular style and is the largest church in Norwich. The 'pepper pot' pinnacles, lead-covered flêche with dainty flying buttresses and parapet were added during restoration towards the end of the 19th century. Because of its close location to the Theatre Royal it has become known as the actor's church.

31

THEN – THEATRE STREET, *c.* **1954**: A popular watering hole for visitors and actors at the Theatre Royal opposite was the Shakespeare p.h., dating back to the early 19th century, on the corner with Lady Lane. Also seen is the Trinity Presbyterian Church, formed in 1866, on St Andrew's Street and later of St Peter's Hall, Theatre Street. Public worship began at this new church designed by Edward Boardman in 1875. In the 'Blitz' of 1942, the whole building apart from the tower was gutted by fire. *CLIVE MANSON COLLECTION*

NOW: A new Presbyterian Church opened in 1956 on the former Baptist Church site in Unthank Road. The remains of the church on Theatre Street were demolished in 1957. The Shakespeare closed in May 1960 and was flattened for the Bethel Street Car Park and the Norwich Central Library, which opened in 1963. The site has now been incorporated into the city's new complex, The Forum. Visible in the distance is the Bethel Hospital founded in 1713 'for the habitation of poor lunatics, and not for natural-born fools or idiots'.

THEN – HAYMARKET, *c.* 1898: On the far left is the 'County & City Supply Stores' dealers in groceries, wines and spirits. The proprietor at the time was Mr Edward Wild, an Alderman and a director of Norwich Union. Mr Wild was also involved in the formation of the CEYMS rooms, nearby on Little Orford Street, later renamed Orford Place. Next door is the Norfolk and Norwich Savings Bank which was built in 1844 'for the beneficial investment of the savings of the humbler classes' and which despite its impressive design would only remain on this site for little over fifty years. The house on the right was once the home of Sir Thomas Browne (1605–1682), the celebrated writer, physician and philosopher, who came to Norwich in 1636. Sir Thomas Browne was knighted by Charles II, in 1671 and was buried in St Peter Mancroft Church. In Hay Hill, a statue was erected by public subscription in 1905 to his memory.

RHODA BUNN COLLECTION

NOW: All those buildings seen standing in 1898 were demolished at the turn of the 20th century to clear a route for the new tram system of 1900. The Savings Bank had to be cleared to remove the sharp bend and thus rounding off the corner and widening the road for the new tram tracks to be laid. The Norfolk and Norwich Savings Bank was relocated to the redeveloped Red Lion Street. Mr Wild sold his grocery business to James Roofe who had new premises designed by George Skipper and erected on the site of the old store and Savings Bank, which still stand today, with the year 1902 inscribed on the stonework. By the 1920s International Stores had taken over the County and City Supply Stores and the property is well-remembered as being a ladies fashion boutique by the name of SNOB in the 1970s and 1980s. These days a sports shop now occupies the premises. On the left of both images can be seen the side entrance to Lamb Inn Yard, home of one of the City's most renowned hostelries, The Lamb Inn, nowadays known as Henrys @ The Lamb.

THEN – GOOSE & GRIDIRON PUBLIC HOUSE, *c. 1898*: Photographed at the junction with Little Orford Street and Rampant Horse Back Street, with Red Lion Street barely visible at the back on the extreme right, this unassuming building had been the unusually named Goose and Gridiron public house. The pub sign, which had hung over the doors was thought to be a parody of the 'Swan and Harp', the London Company of Musicians' coat of arms. The hostelry dated back to the early 19th century and became known as the Orford Stores in 1890. It closed in 1891 when Mr Samuel Cork was the licensee and Colemans Brewery Co Ltd were the brewers of the ale served.

RHODA BUNN COLLECTION

NOW: The area where the Goose and Gridiron stood has had a century of change. Little Orford Street and Rampant Horse Back Street were demolished to clear the way for the tram system of 1900 and became the central hub of the tram system known as Orford Place. Following the cessation of the tram system in 1935, and the 'Blitz' of April 1942, the site was then incorporated into Curl's new department store of the 1950s which is now Debenhams, with a shoe shop, Shoe Zone and the popular sports store of Pilch next door. Red Lion Street is visible in the left-hand distance. It is worth noting that after all these developments and alterations that Orford Place has once again become a narrow thoroughfare, which is open only to pedestrians.

THEN – RED LION STREET, *c.* 1896: Looking towards St Stephen's Plain, a variety of trades were in existence in this unrecognisable scene. On the left, Daniel Price was the fishmonger and game dealer and next door at the old Cricketers' Arms public house, William Hughes, was the landlord. A boot-maker and rope-makers occupied the adjoining gabled buildings. William Clarke, also of 3 Orford Hill, occupied the four-storey building next door, with his ironmongery business. *RHODA BUNN COLLECTION*

NOW: The ramshackle row of buildings were demolished and the street was widened for the tram system of 1900. The new buildings were designed by Norwich architects George Skipper and Edward Boardman and were built in the early years of the 1900s. The Cricketers' Arms relocated to part of the new Anchor Buildings built here and remained until 1959. Restaurants, shoe and fashion shops, a bank, building societies, hairdressers and various offices currently trade along Red Lion Street.

THEN – CASTLE MEADOW, *c.* 1910: Here we see a flock of sheep being driven along, having been purchased from the cattle and livestock market. On the left are the stables of Spelman's Horse Sales, which were held opposite The Bell Hotel until the late 1920s when it moved to Golden Ball Street. The Bell Hotel, dates back to the 15th century, and in the 18th century, The Revolution Club, who embraced the views of the French Revolutionaries, met here, as did The Hell Fire Club. *CLIVE MANSON COLLECTION*

NOW: This up-to-date view illustrates some of the changes that have taken place here over the years. After the closure of the cattle market in 1961, the site was used as car parking until the construction of the Castle Mall shopping centre, which opened in 1993. The Bell Hotel was used as a headquarters and billets for the American Women's Army Corps from 1943–1945. Since its reopening in 1994 by J D Weatherspoon, it has re-established itself as one of the city's most popular pubs, for both locals and tourists, day and night.

THEN – S D PAGE & SONS, HAY HILL: On the left is The Picture House, opened in 1911, which became The Haymarket Picture House in about 1930. The origins of brushmakers S D Page & Sons can be traced back to 1746, when Francis Allen began basket-making here. After his death in 1762, his business was taken over by Samuel Deyns and then by his grandson Samuel Deyns Page in 1803. The brush-making industry flourished and in 1886 a further factory was opened in Wymondham. *BRIDEWELL MUSEUM COLLECTION*

NOW: In 1955 the Haymarket Picture House became The Gaumont and then closed in 1959. A new store was built on the site in 1961. Following a merger in 1920, S D Page & Sons became the Briton Brush Company Ltd and the Haymarket factory closed in 1927 when the whole operation moved to Wymondham. F Lambert & Son Ltd, tea-merchants trading in Norwich since 1843, took over the premises. After demolition in the late 1960s C & A's new store was built in 1970, and has been occupied by Next since 2001.

THEN – GENTLEMEN'S WALK, *c.* 1880: A fine early image of the Market Place with its wooden tables and awnings long before the permanent market was erected. Horse and carriage cabs line this thoroughfare, once known as Nether (Lower) Way. It was renamed after the young dandies of the 18th century who walked here after meeting in their gentlemen's clubs. On the right is The Royal Hotel, on the site of the 15th century Angel Inn, renamed in 1840 in honour of Queen Victoria's marriage.   *TERRY NICHOLLS COLLECTION*

NOW: In 1896 an undertaking was given to close the Royal Hotel on completion and opening of a new hotel, under construction on Bank Plain. In its place George Skipper designed the Royal Arcade, in the Art Nouveau style. The Royal Arcade has since been well-maintained and provides a pleasurable shopping experience, which includes Norwich's very own Colman's Mustard shop. In the 19th century, many different trades occupied the shops here and now pedestrianised it remains at the heart of city centre life.

THEN – LONDON STREET, *p.u.* **1910:** A busy scene taken beside the Market Place. On the left in a former 18th century mansion is Dean & Palmer tailors, Post Office Telephone Offices, Walter Boston, boot and shoe manufacturer, Theodore Rossi, jeweller, and then there is the Corner Tea House. On London Street, beyond Jarrold & Sons Ltd, is John Dodson's grocers' store later the International Stores at the junction with Castle Street. On the right, is the Music Warehouse of W Howlett & Son. *RHODA BUNN COLLECTION*

46

NOW: Modern day shops and services occupy the premises of a century ago on Guildhall Hill. Jarrolds have expanded their department store and have recently acquired the gabled buildings of G Dunn & Co resulting in them occupying the whole block between London Street, Little London Street, Bedford Street and Exchange Street. Burton's menswear store occupies Howlett's Music Warehouse and upon closer inspection it appears that the third storey of the building has been removed at some stage!

THEN – CALEY'S, LONDON STREET: A rarely-seen photograph of I W Caley & Co's high-class silk mercers store with their royal warrant, whose services included costumiers, milliners, outfitters, trousseaux and layettes, which create an evocative and nostalgic image of the era. Out of view, Garlands, general drapers were the occupants of Nos. 13–17 with Godfrey's hosiery warehouse next door at No. 19. Caley's were at Nos. 21 and 23 and had extended to No. 25 by 1912.   *CLIVE MANSON COLLECTION*

NOW: In the 1930s, Garlands extended to No. 19 and Caley's was occupied by Goodways Ltd, house furnishers, and Gardiner & Co, furriers, and later Burtol cleaners. As a result of bomb damage in World War Two, Buntings relocated to Caley's former store from St Stephen's Plain, and by the 1960s Garlands occupied this whole length. On 1 August 1970 a fire destroyed Garlands and a new store was built on the site, which closed in 1984. The property was then divided into four separate retail outlets.

THEN – HARMER'S, ST ANDREW'S STREET: Seen here decorated to celebrate the Silver Jubilee of 1935, F W Harmer & Co, clothing manufacturers were founded in 1825 and occupied the St Andrew's Works, built in the 1890s here, where the Golden Can p.h. had stood. In both World Wars, the factory, made uniforms for the civil and armed services. In World War One they produced two tons of uniforms a day. Thomas Gaffer, a sewing machine dealer, occupied the premises next door. *ERNEST WEBSTER COLLECTION*

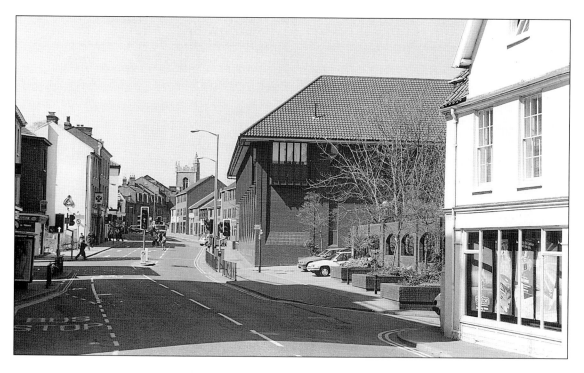

NOW: Hitler got his own back on Harmers, for making British uniforms, when their factory was gutted and destroyed by fire during an air raid on 18 March 1943. The business relocated to Havers Road. The site is now part of the Telephone Exchange with open space to the side and car parking to the rear. The gabled building next to the Harmer's site has survived the years and developers, and has recently become a sales office for Tops Property Services. In the distance, Charing Cross is clearly visible.

THEN – CITY ARMS P.H. *c.* **1898:** At the corner of Princes Street and St Andrew's Hill stood the City Arms, dating back to the 16th century. On the left is Garsett House, which has carvings dating back to 1589. On the right is Thomas Wells & Co, hat and cap makers, whose son H Rumsey Wells became renowned for his stylish designs. Most of what is shown here including the south wing of Garsett House and part of the cap-makers would be flattened in 1898–9 to clear a route for the new tramlines. *RHODA BUNN COLLECTION*

NOW: The cut to Redwell Street exposed the ancient Suckling House, which in 1923–4 Ethel and Helen Colman bought and restored, having the adjoining Stuart Hall built, which they presented to the City in 1925. These premises including the cap-makers, which has lost its third storey, have been converted into Cinema City, opened in 1978, and which includes a restaurant. Currently there are plans to refurbish Cinema City, but this is unlikely to have such a profound effect as the creation of the new road in 1899.

THEN – SOLDIERS AND SAILORS INSTITUTE, TOMBLAND, *c.* 1912: These 19th century buildings were situated on the corner of Queen Street (formerly Red Well Street) and Tombland, and were a home for soldiers and sailors, where Mrs E Jump was the superintendent in 1912. The institute would, by 1922, be occupied by an antique dealer, William Plowright and the adjacent premises seen on Queen Street later became tearooms.

TONY WILLIAMSON COLLECTION

NOW: The tearooms suffered damage from an incendiary bomb in World War Two and the burnt-out shell remained for some years, like many of the war-damaged buildings in the city. With so many rebuilding projects to be worked on, it was inevitable that it would be many years before completion. The old buildings were demolished in 1956 and rebuilt, with estate agents, Haart, currently occupying the corner premises. Many of the businesses in this area of the city centre today, are engaged in the property services market.

THEN – BANK PLAIN, *c.* **1926:** Photographed from outside the General Post Office. With the removal of the glass windows and roof tiles, demolition is already under way on empty offices, once occupied by architects, solicitors, stock and share brokers. John and Henry Gurney founded Gurney's Bank in 1775, in 1777 they moved from Pitt Street to Bank Plain, just out of view. In 1896 they merged with Barclays Bank. Just visible on the right is the Royal Hotel, opened in 1897. *PETER LARTER COLLECTION*

NOW: Castle Meadow was widened in 1926–7 and the County Police Station, once on the left, demolished. Barclays Bank new premises were completed by 1931 from the designs of Edward Boardman & Son and Brierly and Rutherford of York. Early in 2003, the doors of this branch of Barclays Bank closed for the final time. In the summer of 2003, plans were approved to convert the premises into a centre for Norfolk's youth. Recent road works have once again changed the view since our 'up to date' photograph was taken.

THEN – CATTLE MARKET STREET & MARKET AVENUE, *c.* 1905: Photographed across the old cattle market, here is a fine display of harnesses and saddlery made by David Maggs of No. 2 Market Avenue. On the left is the Eagle and Child, a Bullards public house, which closed in 1907. On the right is the Plough Inn, supplied by Morgans brewery, where Miss Eliza Coe was the licensee. This image illustrates the importance of horses and farming to the community in those days. *PETER LARTER COLLECTION*

NOW: In World War Two the Plough Inn was used by the USAAF Military Police. The cattle market moved to Hall Road in 1961 and this area became a shadow of its former self, losing its previous agricultural trade. In 1973, the Plough was named La Rouen, after the city's twin town in France. It closed in the mid-1990s when it was monitored for damage during the construction of the Castle Mall and reopened as Le Rouen. On either side is part of the popular Castle Mall complex with car parking and a multi-screen cinema.

THEN – BER STREET, *c.* **1937:** Photographed at the junction with Finklegate, this display of pride and pageantry is believed to have been taken at the 1937 Coronation Procession, which started at Bracondale Woods. The church of St John de Sepulchre 'the church with a parish of butchers' is just out of view on the right. Across the road on the left, on the corner with Ashbourne Street is the Lily Tavern at Nos. 152 and 154 Ber Street, where William Barber was the landlord. *PETER LARTER COLLECTION*

NOW: Once colloquially referred to as 'Blood and Guts Street' because of the slaughterhouses and butchers' shops there, rather than the regular street fights which took place, this view of Ber Street focuses on the surviving buildings on the far side. The Lily Tavern, a Bullards public house closed on 30 April 1963 and with other 16th and 17th century dwellings, was demolished, but it is still commemorated by Lily Terrace. The buildings next door to the Lily Tavern have thankfully, not met the same fate.

THEN – ABBEY LANE, *c.* **1939:** Known as Cockey Lane until the turn of the 20th century, Abbey Lane lies between King Street and the River Wensum. To the right is the site of the church of St Clement Conesford, which transferred to St Julian's church in 1482. Here we see a cobbled Abbey Lane on the eve of World War Two, and posters advertising Tom Smith's locally-made Christmas crackers and film shows at the Regal on Dereham Road and at the Cinema Palace on Magdalen Street. *CLIVE MANSON COLLECTION*

NOW: The view today has drastically changed, with all the old cottages having long since gone but the curve of the pathway remains. Across the river are the residential flats of the Riverside scheme. The Waterfront, a music venue, is in an old maltings. The folk who lived here remember Abbey Lane for its community spirit and for being the home of the Aldous ice cream factory, Whitbread & Co Ltd bottled beer stores and the former location of the City mortuary until the 1960s.

THEN – ST FAITH'S TAVERN, 17 MOUNTERGATE STREET, *c.* **1912:** The proprietor Mr Oscar Farrow, the licensee here between 1885 and 1920, stands in the doorway of St Faith's Tavern, at the corner with Synagogue Street, opposite the Jewish Synagogue. This was one of many corner pubs in Norwich and was owned by Morgans. There were many trades in existence in this area, including a boot and shoe factory, timber merchants, Boulton & Paul Engineers and Morgans Brewery.

NOW: During the Second World War, the Synagogue opposite was destroyed. St Faith's Tavern closed on 28 August 1961, and was demolished. The land became part of the Morgans Brewery sites of King Street and Synagogue Street. There is no trace of Synagogue Street today, having been entirely lost below the brewery bottle store building, by the end of the 1960s. Brewing ceased here in 1985 and today the land is the Old Brewery Car Park and will hopefully soon be redeveloped as part of St Ann's Wharf.

THEN – PRINCE OF WALES ROAD, AUGUST 1912: Floodwater flows across the junction with Rose Lane, which until the 1860s, had been the main route from Thorpe Station to the city centre. On the left is the Automobile Association & Motor Union office and the Prince of Wales Palace Picture Theatre. In the centre is the Norfolk Railway House p.h., built as a toll house for Foundry Bridge. On the right are O H Rice & Sons, builders, Walter Morris, cycle dealer and George Morris & Sons, carriage & motor builders.

66

NOW: The AA moved after the Great War and the Picture Theatre closed in 1922. In 1942 Coleman & Co Ltd took over the premises and it became Wincarnis House. In the 1950s it was renamed the Grosvenor Rooms, a dance hall where, on 17 May 1963, The Beatles played to an audience of 1700. The Rooms closed later that year to be demolished and replaced with Grosvenor House. The Norfolk Railway House, now the Compleat Angler, is popular with office workers and tourists. On the right, a complex of offices and shops was built in the 1960s.

THEN – GREAT EASTERN HOTEL, *p.u.* 1907: This was built in 1893–4 on adjoining land of the former Great Eastern Hotel. The first Foundry Bridge, taking its name from the Iron Foundry slightly downstream, opened in 1811. In 1844 it was replaced with a larger bridge catering for the increase in traffic from Thorpe Station, and with the construction of Prince of Wales Road, in the 1860s, there was again a need for a new bridge. Work began in 1884 and the new bridge opened in 1888.   *RHODA BUNN COLLECTION*

NOW: The Great Eastern Hotel was demolished in 1963 and construction of a new hotel began in 1969, designed by J Owen Bond & Son. The Hotel Nelson opened on 8 March 1971 being extended in 1985 on an old timber merchant's grounds. A further leisure and bedroom extension on the site of 'Spring Gardens', established in 1739 in the grounds of St Faith's House, opened in 1994. The new Foundry Bridge of 1888 was 5ft wider than intended, which has been useful in providing three traffic lanes at this busy junction.

THEN – RIVERSIDE FROM FOUNDRY BRIDGE, *c.* 1912: Across the River Wensum is the Goods Station adjacent to Thorpe Station, where general goods arriving by train to Norwich would be distributed and loaded for delivery together with the despatch of locally-produced goods leaving the city for other destinations. The church of St John de Sepulchre on Ber Street stands clear against the skyline whilst timber yards and saw mills line the river on the city side next to the Great Eastern Hotel.

NOW: The view is dominated by the Riverside development of recent years, currently offering bars and nightclubs, a multiscreen cinema, ten-pin bowling alley, restaurants, a fitness club, retail stores and residential properties. Whilst the river trade has all but gone this development has rejuvenated the area and businesses are prospering. Providing a glimpse of the past, is the moored Norwich Sea Cadets vessel, soon to be replaced, and the Floating Restaurant. The Hotel Nelson, occupies the city side of the river.

THEN - BARRACK STREET, *c.* 1912: Here is the Boys Brigade parading down a cobbled Barrack Street, with the entrance to Steward & Patteson's Pockthorpe Brewery in the background. On the right next to Horace Nichols' shop is Griffin Yard and the Griffin public house. The name of Barrack Street is derived from the Cavalry Barracks of 1791, located further down the street. Pockthorpe, the area where Barrack Street lies, was once one of the poorest districts in old Norwich. *MR F W BURRAGE COLLECTION*

NOW: Barrack Street is today very different to its narrow predecessor and has been incorporated into the inner link road. In the 1930s, the houses and yards were cleared as part of the slum-clearance programme, with all the premises on the left now demolished. Part of the brewery site has been developed into housing and offices. The Griffin closed in 1930 and on the site The Sportsman was built, opening in 1937, having previously been located on the other side of the road. It closed in 1992 and has been converted into offices.

THEN – GAS WORKS, ST MARTIN-AT-PALACE PLAIN, *c.* **1950:** In the 1800s the use of gas in households, industry and street lamps was becoming increasingly widespread. To complement the existing works at Bishop Bridge, in the 1850s new Gas Works were built here on the site of the manor and grounds of Erpingham House, the 15th century home of Sir Thomas Erpingham, warrior of Agincourt. Between 1920–22, the Works were expanded at a cost of £236,000. *BRIDEWELL MUSEUM COLLECTION*

NOW: Following the conversion to North Sea Gas, the old Gas Works were closed and demolished. In 1981 archaeological excavations on the site revealed the remains of a 12th century house, which would be preserved beneath the new Magistrates' Court, built in 1985. In 1985 however, further excavations could find no trace of Sir Thomas Erpingham's house, which had been thoroughly destroyed in the 1850s. The new Crown Court buildings seen here were constructed in 1987–8.

THEN – TOMBLAND HOUSE, TOMBLAND, *c.* **1896:** Here at Tombland House, on the corner with Wensum Street, at No. 18 Tombland is Edward Gray's linen drapers store, with Mr Gray, or one of his satisfied customers, in the doorway, next to a vast selection of basketware on display for purchase. The sign on the street lamp indicates a Hackney Carriage Stand for seven carriages, a feature indicative of the era. At the turn of the 20th century the ancient and historic coaching inn of the Maid's Head Hotel on Wensum Street extended their premises and incorporated into the existing hotel, the shops at Nos. 1 and 3 Wensum Street of Isaac Buckle and William Mackley hairdresser and Mr Gray's shop on Tombland. When Edward Gray's shop closed he relocated his drapery business to No. 13 Tombland near Tombland Alley. *RHODA BUNN COLLECTION*

NOW: Whilst the Maid's Head dates back to at least the 13th century, it is now quite apparent that this frontage is Mock Tudor, but is nonetheless attractive. Prior to first being recorded as the Mayde's Head in 1472, an inn has stood on the site from at least 1287 and the old coaching inn has also been known as the Molde Fish, the Murtel Fish and Mathilde's Head. In the 18th century, coaches regularly ran from here to London bringing trade and visitors alike and it was in this Golden Age of Coaching that the hostelry enjoyed some of its most notorious occasions including musical evenings, feasts and banquets. It boasted five cockpits, and many gamesters and sportsman met here. In the 19th century, the Maid's Head was the headquarters of The Everlasting Club, a drinking organisation. At the turn of the 20th century, Walter Rye saved the Hotel from a large brewer who intended to commercialise the inn. The Maids Head also now occupies further premises on Tombland, as far as the junction with Palace Street and remains today as one of the city's most popular and impressive hotels with its restaurant and function rooms.

THEN – ELM HILL CORNER, *c.* **1898:** On the corner of Elm Hill and Wensum Street are the premises of George Edwards, located next door to the Turkey Cock public house on Elm Hill, which was owned by Steward & Patteson. George Edwards was one of Norwich's many boot and shoemakers. Next-door to him on Wensum Street is The Grapes' public house where Richard Mallet was the licensee between 1892 and 1903. Adjoining premises were occupied by confectioners, stationers and a barber.   *RHODA BUNN COLLECTION*

NOW: For the tracklaying for the tram system of 1900, this row of buildings was dramatically cut back and some of the restructured buildings refaced with Mock Tudor timbers. The boot shop remains were incorporated into the Turkey Cock, which closed in 1962 and is now Olive's, a delicatessen and coffee shop. Over the years The Grapes has also been known as Backs, the Silver Dollar, the Silver Jubilee, The Lawyer and in 1996, became the Fugitive & Firkin, and is now simply called The Fugitive.

THEN – BUTTERFANTS, FYE BRIDGE STREET, *c. 1898:* Adjacent to the riverside, and a narrow Fye Bridge, is William Butterfants' grocery store with its decorated advertising proudly denoting his premises at No. 2 Fye Bridge Street with L Morris, family butchers next door. George Watson, corn dealer, William England, coal dealer, also occupied premises on Fye Bridge Street and Carter Steward & Co's Wine Vaults were situated in the 16th century merchants' house, next to St Clement's Alley. *RHODA BUNN COLLECTION*

NOW: By 1912, Butterfants had closed; a hosiery knitter, the coal dealer and the Wine Vaults remained. Butterfants and the adjacent property have been demolished, widening the river to alleviate flooding. Fye Bridge was lengthened and widened between 1931–4 to cater for the increase in traffic and provided work for the unemployed. With the first half of the new bridge completed on 1 July 1933, the bridge was officially opened on 29 May 1934. In 1963, Carter Steward & Co's Wine Vaults was renamed The Mischief Tavern.

GREAT FIRE IN NORWICH
SEXTON'S BOOT. FACTORY
DESTROYED JAN.16.1913

THEN – SEXTONS FIRE, FISHERGATE, 1913: Crowds gather on Quayside to look at the smouldering remains of H Sexton & Son's Ltd Boot and Shoe Factory. The fire began in the early hours of 16 January 1913 and Mr William Steward, an employee, raised the alarm, but within minutes the flames had burst through the roof. The factory, having employed 700 men and women, was virtually gutted and the fire was left to burn itself out, with the damage estimated at £100,000.   *PETER LARTER COLLECTION*

NOW: Boot and shoe production was once the city's main trade with *Kelly's Directory* of 1912 listing 63 manufacturers. In 2003 only the offices of Start-rite remain, with production moving overseas. With the River Wensum liable to flooding, in 1924–5 it was widened and the nearby Whitefriars Bridge, rebuilt providing work for the post-war unemployed. Today's view is closer to the river's edge than its predecessor and shows St Edmund's Church and the recently built residential apartments of St Edmund's Wharf.

THEN – COLEGATE STREET & MAGDALEN STREET, *c.* **1898:** The corner store at No. 2 Magdalen Street with a typical display of chemist's bottles, is occupied by North Heigham Drug Co. Ltd, chemists store, with Page Woodcock & Son on its sign. Next-door heading down Magdalen Street is Henry Betts, milliner, George Gutteridge, butcher and Harry Smith, tobacconist. On the wall of the house on the corner of Colegate Street by the grand lamp is an advertisement for Spratts' Dog Food. *RHODA BUNN COLLECTION*

NOW: Superficially on first impressions, it appears that the same shop frontage remains today. However, if the chemist's shop still existed, it would actually be in the middle of the road, whilst the Armed Forces Careers' office actually occupies the remains of the house previously on the left. About 7–8 metres were sliced off the buildings on Magdalen Street for the tram system of 1900. Colegate Street is now simply known as Colegate and on Magdalen Street, some of the earlier buildings have been rebuilt.

THEN – MAGDALEN STREET FLOOD, AUGUST 1912: Once the rain stopped, life tried to regain some form of normality. The trams had ceased to run across the flood-stricken city, and only horse-drawn transport or makeshift boats, were in operation. Here looking towards the city, horses and carts are passing Alderson's boot retailers and the King's Head, a Youngs, Crawshay & Youngs public house, where Charles Nixon was the publican between 1904 and 1935. In the distance is the Golden Dog p.h. run by John Hall.

NOW: Magdalen Street remains full of character with Anglia Square close by, servicing the many folk who live in the mass of terrace houses erected north of the city at the turn of the 20th century. The King's Head is still thriving, having been renovated in the summer of 2003. Most of the upper storeys of the other buildings in the view have survived the developers, with an eclectic variety of ground-floor occupants including fabric, furniture, CD and music shops, a Chinese medical centre and a beauty salon.

THEN – STUMP CROSS, *c.* 1898: The old junction with Botolph Street and Magdalen Street was Stump Cross, and was named after a damaged stone cross which once stood there and it was also known as Guylding Cross in Henry VII's reign. In the centre is Green & Wright's grocers store. By C F Stevens & Son, ironmongers shop on Magdalen Street, road works are in progress – nothing changes! The right-hand gabled building is the Queen Victoria, a Lacon's public house run by Thomas Mann. *RHODA BUNN COLLECTION*

NOW: Green & Wright's store became a branch of Barclays Bank by the 1920s. In 1959 an operation commenced, funded by the Civic Trust, whose chairman was Duncan Sandys MP, which gave Magdalen Street a 'face-lift'. It was claimed to be a great success for traders and shoppers alike. However, Botolph Street and Stump Cross including Barclays Bank and the Queen Victoria public house were obliterated in the late 1960s to create the Anglia Square development and the flyover of the early 1970s.

ST. AUGUSTINE'S GATE AND SCHOOL, NORWICH

THEN – ST AUGUSTINE'S SCHOOLS, *c.* **1933:** St Augustine's Council Schools were situated by St Augustine's Gate on the corner of Green Hills and Infirmary Road, now known as Aylsham Road and Waterloo Road respectively. Designed by John Patience, a city surveyor and architect, it was built in the 1870s, in the gothic style. It were one of the first of its kind in Norwich and consisted of three separate buildings, educating girls, boys and infants. In the distance is Henry J Bishop's footwear shop.

NOW: In the destructive air raids of April 1942, the schools suffered a direct hit from a 500kg bomb and the buildings were destroyed. The remains were flattened later that year. Construction of the Norwich Swimming Baths commenced in 1959 on part of the site, and was completed in 1961. After structural problems related to the use of asbestos cement were discovered, demolition commenced in September 1997. In 2002, flats and shops were built on the site. Bishop's old shop is now Wensum Properties.

THEN – ST MARY'S BAPTIST CHURCH, DUKE STREET, 1942: This picture taken by George Swain just four minutes after an air raid on 19 October 1942 shows the destruction with which folk lived during World War Two. The church on St Mary's Plain was founded in 1745 and a new church was built in 1810 and enlarged in 1839 and 1886. Damaged by fire in 1939, firebombs gutted the church interior in the spring of 1942 and then in October the remaining chapel walls were destroyed. *GEORGE SWAIN COLLECTION*

NOW: On VE Day a Thanksgiving Service took place here, where 300–400 people prayed in the church's ruined grounds. The congregation then worshipped at Stuart Hall and later at the school in Duke Street. The foundation stone of St Mary's Baptist Church was laid on 5 July 1951. Stanley J Wearing designed the new church with construction taking place in 1951–2. The church has recently decided to merge with Dereham Road Baptist Church and will vacate this site. On the left is a high-class car-sales office.

GREAT FLOOD AT NORWICH. AUGUST 27 & 28 1912. OAK STREET.

PIONEER SERIES

THEN – OAK STREET, 1912 FLOODS: Here children pose for the photographer in the floodwaters. On the left by Talbot Yard is Edmund Barker's barbers with a shop next to Dog Yard. The usual variety of trades of the period occupied the remaining premises of mostly 17th century origin. In the distance is the White Lion public house and on the far side of the junction of Station Road is St Martin's at Oak Mission Hall. The Jolly Skinners' public house, with Edward Brandish as the landlord, is on the right.

NOW: The Norwich Amenities Preservation Society acquired the gabled buildings on the left in 1938 and the Norwich Preservation Trust in 1971 again saved them. They are all well kept and stand adjacent to St Crispin's Road, part of the inner link road of the early 1970s, which cut Oak Street into two. The White Lion was once the Tap & Spile and has been the Old White Lion since 1997. On the right there have been changes as some of the old properties are now the forecourts of a mouldings firm and a funeral home.

THEN – SWAN LAUNDRY, HEIGHAM STREET: The Norwich Steam Laundry & Baths Co Ltd, were established in 1875. Previously housewives had to rely on the local washerwoman but as time progressed these steam-driven purpose-built laundries took over. In 1879, swimming baths had been built attached to these premises and in 1902 the company became known as the Swan Laundry and leased out the baths. The Swan Swimming Club was formed at the swimming baths in 1880. *BRIDEWELL MUSEUM COLLECTION*

NOW: The Swan Swimming Club continued to use the pool until its closure in 1933. The Swan Laundry remained here until at least the mid-1970s and Herrells (Norwich) Ltd, steel stockholders, then occupied the site. In recent years the buildings were demolished and a residential housing complex built on the site. This is a busy route for traffic with Waterworks' Road in the distance. On the right is the junction with Mile Cross Road, which had been built in 1923 as part of an unemployment relief scheme.

Norwich Floods, August 27/12. Barn Road & Westwick Street. No. J. & S. 7797.

THEN – BARN ROAD AND WESTWICK STREET, AUGUST 1912 FLOODS: Here, youngsters are wading across the floodwaters as residents watch. On the corner of Westwick Street, at No. 76 Barn Road, is George Fisher's tobacconist's shop. In the right-hand distance, is A & W Cushion, timber merchants. Other premises on the right include Albert Cooper, confectioner, The Railway Coffee House dining rooms run by Ernest Smith and, just visible on the corner with Heigham Street, is the Rose & Thistle public house.

NOW: The Roman Catholic Cathedral, built between 1884 and 1910, towers over the view towards Grapes Hill. With the construction of the inner link road, Barn Road was virtually doubled in width to create the dual carriageway. On the left at the junction with Westwick Street is The Cathedral Retail Park whilst across the thoroughfare, on the right, the extensive St Benedict's Sawmills of A & W Cushion Limited are still in existence, and their premises are clearly visible, due to the road layout.

THEN – WINCARNIS WORKS, WESTWICK STREET: Coleman & Co Ltd, were founded prior to the 20th century. In the 1890s they took over premises in Westwick Street and in January 1912 these new buildings were opened. Their most famous product was Wincarnis; 'The Great Tonic Restorative – recommended by thousands of the medical profession. Over 8,000 testimonials received'. The footwear factories of Hale Bros, and Morgan Bros were either side of the Works. *PETER LARTER COLLECTION*

NOW: In the Blitz of April 1942, the Works were destroyed and relocated. After the war, Coleman's returned to Westwick Street, having already bought adjoining properties for a new factory. As well as bottling wines and importing brandy and port, they made jellies, Vitacup and Odol Toothpaste, but were taken over by Reckitt & Colman in the late 1960s who eventually sold the Wincarnis business. Wincarnis Tonic Wine was still made here in the 1970s. The Cathedral Retail Park and car park now occupies the site.

THEN – ST GILES' GATE, *c.* 1906: Seen looking towards the city with tram No. 31 on its travels, St Giles' Street has many fine Georgian buildings and during the 18th and 19th centuries it was the residential area of many celebrated doctors. On the left can be seen the shops belonging to Joseph English, chemists, Davison Bros, fruiterers, and Herbert & Miller, fancy drapers. In the distance is St Giles' Church whilst on the right is the St Giles' Gates Stores public house, owned by Cooper, Brown & Co.

NOW: The St Giles' Gates Stores closed its doors for the final time on 8 December 1964 following a compulsory purchase for the forthcoming road improvement scheme. On the left the premises of a chemists, fruiterers and electrical engineers, whilst on the right, a butchers, a tobacconists and the public house were all demolished to clear the way for the inner link road completed in the early 1970s. This junction has altered drastically, with a footbridge and a constant flow of traffic beneath it.

THEN – ROSE VALLEY, UNTHANK ROAD, *c.* 1898: Children gather to pose for the photographer, next to the unadopted road of Rose Valley and by William Lydamore's general store with a fine display of pails and wash baths attached to the railings. The house next-door at No. 107 was a private residence whilst No. 105 was Misses J & H Watts' Day School. Beyond here were a combination of private residences and businesses. *RHODA BUNN COLLECTION*

NOW: Nowadays Unthank Road is a busy road linking up to the inner ring road. The Grapevine, wine merchants, with the shop front having been extended, now occupies the general store. The private house next door is now a video & DVD store. The school and all the adjacent houses have had their well-tended gardens cleared to make way for the forecourts to the various businesses and shops. It is quite apparent just how much shorter these forecourts are following widening of the road.

THEN – NEWMARKET ROAD: Norwich City played at Newmarket Road from their foundation in 1902 until moving to 'The Nest' in 1908. The first match here was on 6 September 1902 and was a friendly, against Harwich & Parkeston with 2,000 spectators, which City drew 1–1. This picture was taken during the game against West Ham in October 1905, which City won 1–0, playing in their blue and white halves. In the background is the old pavilion, which backed onto what is now Daniels Road. *PAUL STANDLEY COLLECTION*

NOW: This current view of the Newmarket Road ground is taken looking in the opposite direction to show the current pavilion. The old pavilion survived through until the 1990s when it was demolished. The ground is still used as a sports field by the Town Close House Preparatory School. One wonders if the children playing there today realise that the 'forefathers' of their current Norwich City heroes once played week in and week out on that very grass a hundred years ago.

THE NEST.

NORWICH CITY FOOTBALL GROUND. Aug : 08

Copyright

THEN – THE NEST: When the Canaries looked for a new home in 1908 they built their very own 'Nest' on a filled-in chalk pit, known as 'Ruymp's Hole'. Legendary for its 50ft-high concrete retaining wall, this view looks west to Rosary Road and the city centre. Here in August 1908, a month before the first game was played on 1 September against Fulham which City won 2–1 in front of 3,300 fans, there still seems to be much work to do. The five houses to the right were later demolished to make way for club facilities.

NOW: The final match played at The Nest was on 6 May 1935. The Canaries opponents were Arsenal in the Hospital Cup which City won 1–0 in front of a 15,500 capacity crowd. The view today shows that some of the terraced houses still remain and the view over the fine City of Norwich remains just as impressive. The ground is now home to the imposing warehouse of Bertram Books, a book wholesaler, who obviously found good use for the site and can truly boast that their warehouse is 'the size of a football pitch'!

THEN – CARROW ROAD: In May 1935, the F.A. informed Norwich City that the Nest was no longer considered adequate for professional football. The Canaries decided on new premises in Carrow Road, home of the Boulton and Paul Sports Club. Work began at 3.45am (!) on 11 June and here is the Main Stand under construction. By 31 August, 82 days later, a modern stadium had been completed and the ground was ready for business, when 29,779 spectators roared City on to a 4–3 victory against West Ham.